AUGUST 15 - NOVEMBER 15, 1998

GERALD PETERS GALLERY, 1011 PASEO DE PERALTA, SANTA FE, NEW MEXICO

NOVEMBER 21 - DECEMBER 23, 1998

GERALD PETERS GALLERY, 2913 FAIRMOUNT, DALLAS, TEXAS

PICASSO ON PAPER

SELECTED WORKS FROM THE MARINA PICASSO COLLECTION

PICASSO ON PAPER

SELECTED WORKS FROM THE MARINA PICASSO COLLECTION

AUGUST 15 - NOVEMBER 15, 1998
GERALD PETERS GALLERY, 1011 PASEO DE PERALTA, SANTA FE, NEW MEXICO
NOVEMBER 21 - DECEMBER 23, 1998
GERALD PETERS GALLERY, 2913 FAIRMOUNT, DALLAS, TEXAS

© COPYRIGHT 1998 GERALD PETERS GALLERY, INC.
ALL WORKS OF PABLO PICASSO ©1998 ESTATE OF PABLO PICASSO/ARTISTS RIGHTS SOCIETY (ARS), NEW YORK.
CERTAIN OTHER ILLUSTRATIONS ARE COVERED BY CLAIMS TO COPYRIGHT LISTED IN THE PHOTOGRAPH CREDITS.
ALL RIGHTS RESERVED. NO PART OF THIS PUBLICATION MAY BE REPRODUCED OR TRANSMITTED IN ANY FORM OR BY ANY MEANS,
ELECTRONIC OR MECHANICAL, INCLUDING PHOTOCOPYING, RECORDING, OR INFORMATION STORAGE OR RETRIEVAL SYSTEM,
WITHOUT PERMISSION IN WRITING FROM THE PUBLISHERS.
ISBN: 0-935037-82-9

EXHIBITION AND CATALOGUE DIRECTION: AMY SCOTT
CATALOGUE DESIGN: LAURA MCCURDY
PHOTOGRAPHY: DAN MORSE AND EMILY GOLDEN
PRINTING: WOODS LITHOGRAPHICS, PHOENIX, AZ

COVER: *NU DEBOUT, LES PIEDS DANS L'EAU*, 1920, PENCIL ON PAPER, 9 1/4 X 4 1/2 INCHES (23 X 11.5 CM)
MARINA PICASSO COLLECTION (INVENTORY NUMBER 02935). COURTESY JAN KRUGIER GALLERY, NEW YORK.

WITH AN ESSAY BY JOHN RICHARDSON

PICASSO ON PAPER

SELECTED WORKS FROM THE MARINA PICASSO COLLECTION

ACKNOWLEDGMENTS

The inaugural exhibition of the newly constructed Gerald Peters Gallery in Santa Fe, *Picasso on Paper: Selected Works from the Marina Picasso Collection* represents the realization of a long-standing dream of mine. The first Picasso exhibition of a comprehensive scope to come to Santa Fe, it is comprised primarily of works from the collection of Mme. Marina Picasso, the artist's grand-daughter. Mme. Picasso's generosity is legendary, and I am grateful for being allowed the opportunity to bring her collection to New Mexico. I am also indebted to my friend and colleague Jan Krugier, the exclusive agent of the Marina Picasso Collection. His ongoing support and counsel have been invaluable, and his curatorial assistance with this project has resulted in a diverse group of works that represents the extensive and profound nature of Picasso's genius. In a similar capacity, I would also like to acknowledge Eugene V. Thaw, whose trusted advice I have sought for many years. The exhibition has been further complemented by the generous contributions of Michelle and Herbert Rosenfeld of the Michelle Rosenfeld Gallery, New York, and Desmond Corcoran of the Lefevre Gallery in London. The heartfelt and poignant catalogue essay was contributed by Picasso's friend and biographer, John Richardson.

Picasso on Paper: Selected Works from the Marina Picasso Collection was made possible through the collaborative efforts of the Gerald Peters Gallery, Santa Fe, and the Jan Krugier Gallery, New York. My special thanks go to Tzila Krugier, director, and Carrie Hamilton of the Jan Krugier Gallery for their insight, dedication, and attention to every aspect of the exhibition, and also to Mme. Ingeborg Weber and the staff of the Galerie Jan Krugier, Ditesheim & Cie in Geneva. Of the Gerald Peters Gallery, I would like to thank Amy Scott, who oversaw the exhibition and the catalogue, which Laura McCurdy designed with sensitivity to the presentation of Picasso's graphic work. Our photographer, Dan Morse, documented the works for the catalogue, and gallery registrar Meredith Nix coordinated all domestic shipping. It is through the fine efforts of all of these people that we have at last brought Pablo Picasso, the most prodigious artist of the twentieth century, to Santa Fe – a city long recognized for its outstanding tradition of creative excellence.

GERALD P. PETERS III

FOREWORD

It is with great pleasure that I present this comprehensive group of works on paper by Pablo Picasso (1881 - 1973). The most prolific artist in the history of western art, throughout his long life Picasso produced an immense body of work that is astonishing in its diversity and creative vitality. As putting his pencil to paper was as necessary to life as his breath, Picasso's drawings are the foundations of all that he accomplished. Accordingly, they are among his most important works. In the raw mediums of pencil, pastel, ink, gouache, and watercolor we can now see fresh the subtle harmonies of his finished oils. Many drawings were created independently of his paintings, are considered to be masterpieces unto themselves.

Picasso was well known for drawing with any medium that was available on any receptive surface. His ability to effortlessly combine graphite, ink, gouache, and watercolor into fluid, cohesive compositions remains unrivaled by any artist of this century. Equally important is his use of line, which shifts effortlessly between classical restraint and baroque energy. Seemingly spontaneous and lucid, at times Picasso's line betrays the careful deliberation and profound intellect that was at the heart of his life's work The sheer diversity among his drawings offers further evidence of the genius inherent within them; in their striking sincerity, they reveal the many sides of their creator. Among the various roles he adopted throughout his life, it is perhaps Picasso the inventor that is best reflected in the present collection. From the cub st still lifes and portraits to the classical nudes, it is possible to detect several visual languages, evidence of his incalculable influence on the development of twentieth century art.

Picasso merged his art with his life, subjecting form to the full range of his emotional and intellectual powers. The self-proclaimed enemy of style, among his innovations was his adaptation of the arbitrary rather than the artful as a means of interpreting his experiences. Today we can search his works for evidence of these stimuli, these sparks of creativity, in an attempt to derive meaning. D. H. Kahnweiler, Picasso's friend and primary dealer for much of his career, felt that through this process, art came into its existence as such. However, as is the case with much that is new in art, Picasso's work was subject to public incomprehension for many years after its creation. After considerable time and the deliberate studies of numerous curators, scholars, collectors, and dealers, Picasso and his work are now widely appreciated and revered as genius. Indeed, he has become emblematic of the spirit of restlessness, change, and innovation that distinguishes the art of this century from that of the past.

GERALD P. PETERS III

IN MEMORY OF PABLITO

Marina Picasso, who inherited most of the drawings in the present show from her grandfather, differs from the artist's other five heirs in that she has made a point of exhibiting as much as possible of her magnificent collection in a succession of traveling exhibitions. If Marina has also sold more of her holdings than the others, it has been for the best of reasons. She has several hundred children to support and the memory of her beloved brother Pablito, who committed suicide in 1973, to perpetuate. The story of how all this came about is as disturbing as it is heartening.

Marina and Pablito Picasso.
Photo courtesy Mme. Marina Picasso.

Marina is the second child of Picasso's only legitimate son and heir, Paulo, and his first wife Emilienne Lotte. As she recounts in her fascinating book, *Les Enfants du Bout du Monde*, Marina and her elder brother Pablito had a nightmarish childhood at the hands of their irresponsible parents: a mother who was violent and vindictive, a father who was a nice enough man but exceedingly weak: a victim of his parents' marital mayhem. Paulo had been overprotected by the neurotic Russian mother he came to loathe, and repeatedly rejected by the all-powerful father he resented yet revered. As a young man, he had aspired to be a racing bicyclist or motorist, but ended up as chauffeur to *le père* as he always called Picasso. *Le père* had no patience with Paulo's chronic alcoholism, even less with his insistence on marrying the "unsuitable" and unstable Emilienne. When the marriage turned out to be even more of a disaster than people had predicted – it ended in less than three years – Emilienne and her children received minimal legal support. Picasso's only contribution was to pay Marina and Pablito's tuition fees at a private lycée, twelve kilometers away from where they lived. Marina says that the money would have been better spent on food. Since they bore the Picasso name, nobody believed they were penniless. Their father was too terrified of *his* father to plead their case; and by the time they were twelve and thirteen, family history was repeating itself. Just as Paulo had fallen from favor by virtue of being the hated Olga's son, and just as Claude and Paloma had suffered a similar fate, by virtue of being Françoise Gilot's children, Marina and Pablito would now have to atone for *their* mother's shortcomings: banished for good, like their uncle and aunt, from their grandfather's presence. Marina holds their step-mother, the artist's second wife Jacqueline, responsible for this edict.

In 1955, Olga Picasso, from whom the artist was separated but not divorced, died. Under French law her only son Paulo was entitled to his mother's half share of her husband's estate. However, for fear of upsetting his father, he never asserted his rights, and so the plight of his children remained as dire as ever. In 1962, Paulo would marry again, the charming and attractive Christine Pauplin, who had already borne him a son, Bernard. Picasso's preference for Christine and her baby meant that Pablito and Marina had less access than ever to their grandfather. Pablito, who was extremely sensitive, took this neglect to heart. He became morose, avoided his friends and vanished for days at a time. In despair at Picasso's continued rejection of him, he drew attention to his plight by spending the night in a sleeping bag outside Nôtre Dame de Vie, the artist's house at Mougins.

On another occasion, August 1972, Pablito broke into Nôtre Dame de Vie, carrying a banner declaring his intention of remaining there until his grandfather agreed to see him. Jacqueline apparently set the dogs on him and called the police, who threw his *motocyclette* into a ditch. When I asked Jacqueline why she had not let Pablito into the house, she claimed he was "crazy". She said she could not allow anyone to distract Picasso from his work. Meanwhile, Marina had also been rebuffed. She aspired to be a doctor, and had applied, through family lawyers, for funds that would enable her to attend medical school. Inevitably, she was turned down, which added to her brother's chagrin. Instead of studying medicine, Marina decided to look after handicapped children — a decision that would change the course of her life.

The day after Picasso's death on April 8, 1973, Pablito returned once again to Nôtre Dame de Vie in the hope of paying his last respects to his grandfather. Once again he was ejected. Even more shocking, his father, now head of the family, went along with Jacqueline's insistence that neither Marina nor any other of the artist's children and grandchildren be allowed to attend the funeral. They had to watch it from a distant vantage-point. These successive rejections broke what was left of Pablito's spirit. The day after the funeral, he swallowed a bottle of bleach, which burned away his intestines. Marina describes finding her brother hemmoraging on the kitchen floor. Pablito took three excruciating months to die. His father, who was admittedly in very poor health, never came to see him, never provided any financial help. The only member of Picasso's entourage to raise a finger was the artist's former mistress Marie-Thérèse Walter, who had taken pity on Emilienne. Although Marie-Thérèse's means were limited, she set about selling some of the drawings Picasso had given her in the hope of saving Pablito, but it was too late. In the end, the parents of one of Pablito's school friends paid for his funeral. Marina felt too resentful ever to see her father again. He died of liver cancer two years later – too soon to benefit from his prodigious inheritance.

Back row, left to right: Gaël, Marina, Flore, front row, left to right, Dimitri, May, Florian. Photo courtesy Mme. Marina Picasso.

Paulo's death meant that Marina became one of six heirs to Picasso's estate. Since she had not as yet received any money, her uncle Claude, who had assumed control of the family's affairs, paid her fare to Paris so that she could attend the lawyers' meetings. The estate took seven years to settle. In 1980, Marina and her half brother Bernard wound up sharing 5/8ths of what was left, after the French state had taken its share for the future Musée Picasso in lieu of inheritance taxes, and Jacqueline had taken her quarter share as a widow. Marina's and Bernard's shares were more than double what the three illegitimate children Claude, Paloma and Maya, each received.

Unlike the other heirs, Marina also received the right to additional paintings, drawings, and sculptures from the estate. Marina was given this privilege because she had never received anything from Picasso during his lifetime. Before the actual share-out took place, each of the beneficiaries was allowed to pick out specific works of personal or sentimental value. Picasso's enormous accumulation of paintings, drawings, sculptures, prints and ceramics was then divided into a great many separate "parcels", varying in size but equivalent in value, for which the heirs proceeded to draw lots. Realizing that she knew little about the value of her grandfather's work, Marina had the good sense to seek expert advice. Jan Krugier, the Geneva dealer who had helped Marie-Thérèse Walter when she came to Pablito's rescue, was the obvious choice. Krugier not only masterminded Marina's selection; he has continued to act as her agent. He has also arranged for portions of her vast and varied collection to tour the world. As Marina says, "despite the resentment I felt for my grandfather, I owe this to his memory". And for students of modern art in cities which have never seen a Picasso retrospective, these exhibitions have been a revelation.

It has taken Marina many years — "*mes années noires*", she says — to exorcise the pain of Pablito's suicide. At first she could not bear even to see the treasures she had inherited, let alone hang any of them on her walls. Everything remained in storage in Paris. But after moving to Switzerland to escape an abusive relation-ship with the father of her two children, she underwent prolonged analysis and managed to put her life together again. She also came to accept her inheritance as a force for good rather than "a burden". Marina had wanted to adopt more children, but her efforts met with no success. In the end, after failing to adopt a Thai child, she was directed to an orphanage in Ho Chi Minh City, Vietnam.

War had left the orphanage overcrowded, underfunded and very dilapidated. Malnutrition was rife. Marina was so moved by the plight of the kids she found there that she decided to take action. Here was a cause worthy of Pablito's memory. Vietnamese officials were very cooperative. Within three months Marina signed the protocols and made the necessary arrangements. Little more than a year later (June, 1991), she was able to inaugurate *Le Village de la Jeunesse de Thu Duc*, a self-sufficient village big enough to house 365 children. She went on to build clinics, schools, holiday homes, and facilities for training the children after they left at the age of fifteen. In 1995, she embarked on yet another pro-ject: an agricultural settlement at Kontum, five hundred miles to the north, for children whose parents are lepers and therefore not allowed to look after them. Marina is also starting up centers that will provide care and shelter to some of the 25,000 orphaned or abandoned children, who roam the streets of Ho Chi Minh City.

To support these ambitious schemes, Marina has been obliged to liquidate part of her collection. On her behalf Krugier puts small groups of Picassos on the market every year. However, she has retained any works that pertain to her own circumstances or predilections. On occasion she has even bought back drawings or paintings that have a special significance for her. Besides works of art, Marina's inheritance included the grandiose villa, Le Californie, back of Cannes, which her grandfather had acquired in 1954. She has now totally refurbished the house and lives there happily with her five children, three of whom she adopted in Vietnam. A magnificent portrait of her grandmother Olga – the one family member she loved, not least because she, too, had a raw deal from the artist – has pride of place in the living room which was once Picasso's studio. Marina has finally been able to exorcise her demons.

JOHN RICHARDSON

PLATES

FIGURE 1

CHANTEUSE (RECTO)

1899-1900, PASTEL ON PAPER, 6 1/4 X 3 1/2 INCHES (16.5 X 9.5 CM).

MARINA PICASSO COLLECTION (INVENTORY NUMBER 00245)

COURTESY JAN KRUGIER GALLERY, NEW YORK

TÊTE D'ESPAGNOLE (VERSO)

1899-1900, PASTEL ON PAPER, 6 1/4 X 3 1/2 INCHES (16.5 X 9.5 CM)

MARINA PICASSO COLLECTION (INVENTORY NUMBER 00245)

COURTESY JAN KRUGIER GALLERY, NEW YORK

FIGURE 3

FEMME AU CHAPEAU À PLUME

1919, GOUACHE ON PAPER, 6 1/2 X 4 1/4 INCHES (16.5 X 11 CM)

MARINA PICASSO COLLECTION (INVENTORY NUMBER 02556)

COURTESY JAN KRUGIER GALLERY, NEW YORK

FIGURE 4

GUÉRIDON ET GUITARE

1920, GOUACHE ON PAPER, 10 7/8 X 8 1/4 INCHES (27.5 X 21 CM)

MARINA PICASSO COLLECTION (INVENTORY NUMBER 02787)

COURTESY JAN KRUGIER GALLERY, NEW YORK

FIGURE 5

NATURE MORTE AU GUÉRIDON

1920, JUAN-LES-PINS, OIL ON CANVAS, 45 3/4 X 28 1/2 INCHES (119 X 76 CM)

MARINA PICASSO COLLECTION (INVENTORY NUMBER 12249)

COURTESY JAN KRUGIER GALLERY, NEW YORK

FEMME ASSISE

1920, JUAN-LES-PINS, GOUACHE, 10 3/4 X 8 3/8 INCHES (27.3 X 21.3 CM)

PRIVATE COLLECTION

FIGURE 10

HOMME AU BERET (LE MARIN)

1946, WATERCOLOR, 19 3/4 X 13 INCHES (50.5 X 33 CM)

PRIVATE COLLECTION

FIGURE 13

TÊTES D'HOMME ET DE FEMME

1970, FELT PEN ON PAPER, 11 X 8 1/2 INCHES (27.5 X 21 CM)

PRIVATE COLLECTION

FIGURE 16

FEMME ET FLEURS

1971, PENCIL AND RED CRAYON ON PAPER, 14 5/8 X 12 5/8 INCHES (37 X 32 CM)

COURTESY JAN KRUGIER GALLERY, NEW YORK.

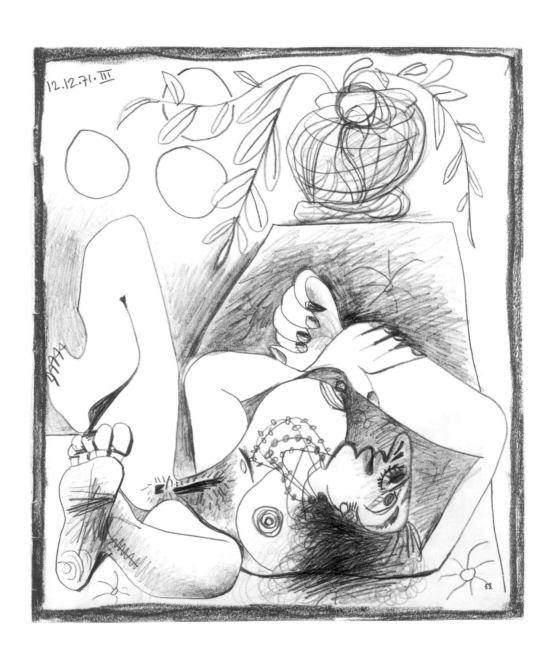

FIGURE 18

PORTRAIT DE PACO SANCHA (RECTO)

1901, INK WASH ON PAPER, 14 3/8 X 9 7/8 INCHES (36.5 X 25.5 CM)

MARINA PICASSO COLLECTION (INVENTORY NUMBER 00475)

COURTESY JAN KRUGIER GALLERY, NEW YORK

FEMME NUE (VERSO)

1901, CHARCOAL ON PAPER, 14 3/8 X 9 7/8 INCHES (36.5 X 25.5 CM)

MARINA PICASSO COLLECTION (INVENTORY NUMBER 00475)

COURTESY JAN KRUGIER GALLERY, NEW YORK.

FIGURE 19

NU COUCHÉ (RECTO)

1901, CONTÉ CRAYON ON PAPER, 12 5/8 X 10 5/8 NCHES (32.5 X 27 CM)

MARINA PICASSO COLLECTION (INVENTORY NUMBER 00476)

COURTESY JAN KRUGIER GALLERY, NEW YORK

DEUX ÉTUDES DE DANSEUSES (VERSO)

1901, INDIA INK ON PAPER, 12 5/8 X 10 5/8 INCHES (32.5 X 27 CM)

MARINA PICASSO COLLECTION (INVENTORY NUMBER 00476)

COURTESY JAN KRUGIER GALLERY, NEW YORK

FIGURE 20

PORTRAIT DE JEUNE FILLE

1903, PENCIL ON PAPER, 12 5/8 X 8 5/8 INCHES (32 X 22 CM)

PRIVATE COLLECTION

Picasso

FIGURE 22

NU

1908-1909, INDIA INK ON PAPER, 12 5/8 X 9 1/2 INCHES (32 X 24 CM)

MARINA PICASSO COLLECTION (INVENTORY NUMBER 01095)

COURTESY JAN KRUGIER GALLERY, NEW YORK

1665 PP

FIGURE 29

ETUDE POUR UN PORTRAIT DE FEMME ASSISE (RECTO)

1915-1916, PARIS, PENCIL ON PAPER, 12 1/4 X 7 1/2 INCHES (31 X 19 CM)

MARINA PICASSO COLLECTION (INVENTORY NUMBER 02426)

COURTESY JAN KRUGIER GALLERY, NEW YORK

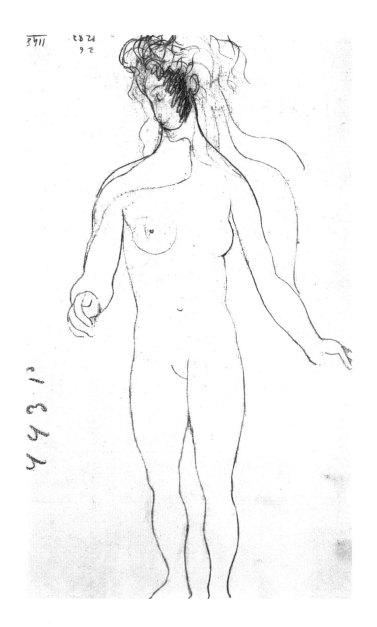

NU DEBOUT (VERSO)

1915-1916, PARIS, PENCIL ON PAPER, 12 1/4 X 7 1/2 INCHES (31 X 19 CM)

MARINA PICASSO COLLECTION (INVENTORY NUMBER 02426)

COURTESY JAN KRUGIER GALLERY, NEW YORK

FIGURE 30

NU DEBOUT, LES PIEDS DANS L'EAU

1920, PENCIL ON PAPER, 9 1/4 X 4 1/2 INCHES (23 X 11.5 CM)

MARINA PICASSO COLLECTION (INVENTORY NUMBER 02935)

COURTESY JAN KRUGIER GALLERY, NEW YORK

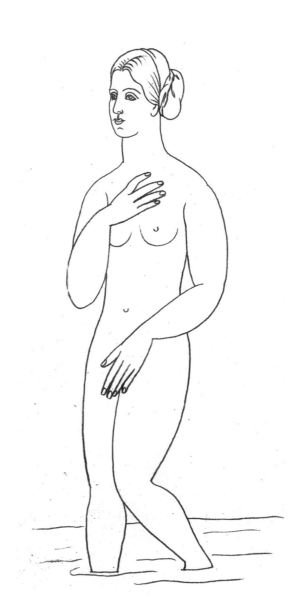

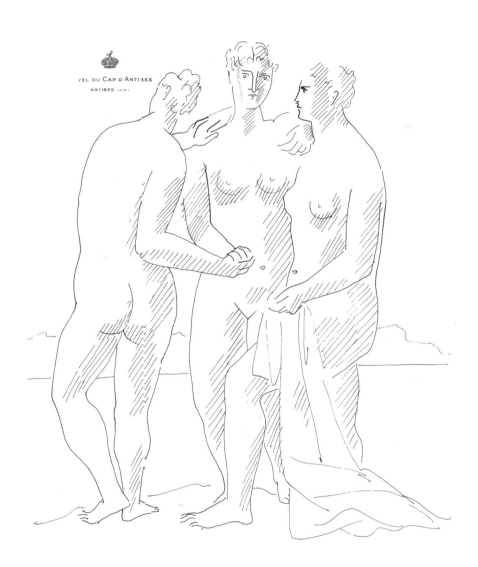

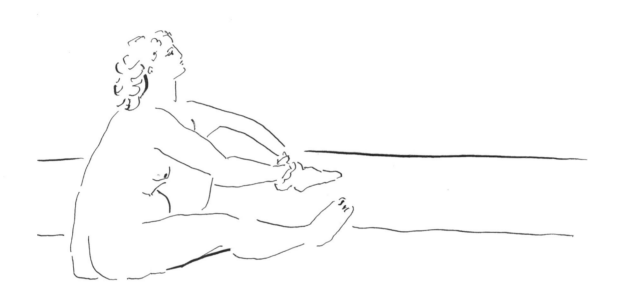

FIGURE 33

BAIGNEUSES (CARNET 67, P. 7)

1923, INDIA INK ON PAPER, 10 3/8 X 14 3/8 INCHES (26.5 X 36.5 CM)

MARINA PICASSO COLLECTION (INVENTORY NUMBER 08731)

COURTESY JAN KRUGIER GALLERY, NEW YORK

FIGURE 34

BAIGNEUSES (CARNET 67, P. 8)

1923, INDIA INK ON PAPER, 10 3/8 X 14 3/8 INCHES (26.5 X 36.5 CM)

MARINA PICASSO COLLECTION (INVENTORY NUMBER 08732)

COURTESY JAN KRUGIER GALLERY, NEW YORK

FIGURE 37

ETUDE POUR LYSISTRATA–DIVERS PERSONNAGES

1933, PENCIL ON PAPER, 7 1/2 X 10 5/8 INCHES (19 X 27 CM)

MARINA PICASSO COLLECTION (INVENTORY NUMBER 03598)

COURTESY JAN KRUGIER GALLERY, NEW YORK

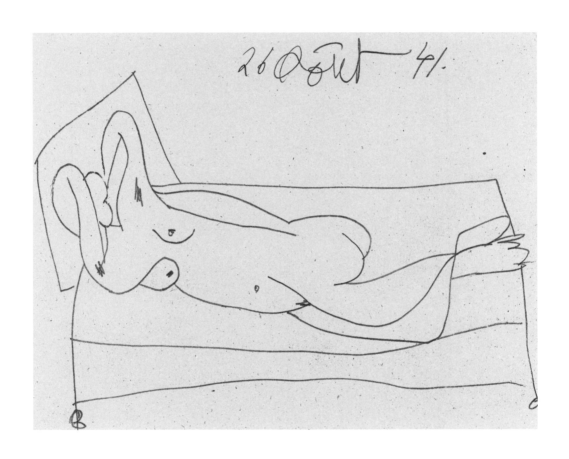

FIGURE 41

FEMME ALLONGÉE SUR UN LIT

1941, PENCIL ON PAPER, 8 1/4 X 10 5/8 INCHES (21 X 27 CM)

MARINA PICASSO COLLECTION (INVENTORY NUMBER 04234)

COURTESY JAN KRUGIER GALLERY, NEW YORK

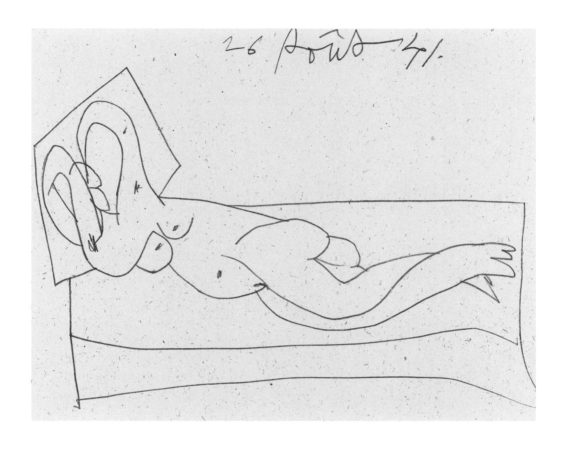

FIGURE 42

NU

1946, PENCIL ON PAPER, 26 1/8 X 19 7/8 INCHES (66.5 X 50.5 CM)

MARINA PICASSO COLLECTION (INVENTORY NUMBER 04942)

COURTESY JAN KRUGIER GALLERY, NEW YORK

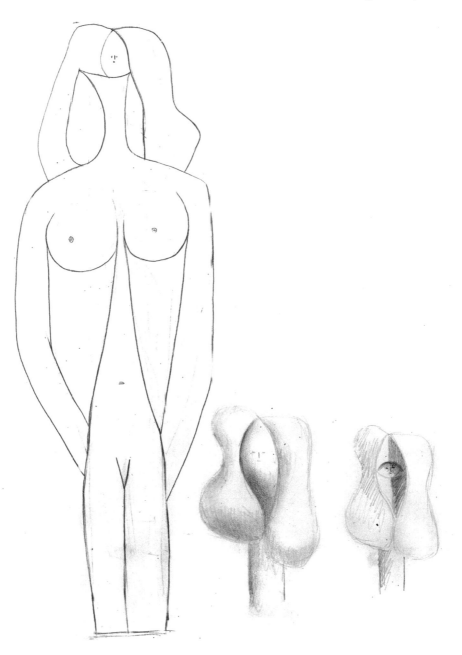

30.12.40.

FIGURE 43

PORTRAIT

1950, PENCIL ON PAPER, 25 3/4 X 19 7/8 INCHES (65.5 X 50.5 CM)

MARINA PICASSO COLLECTION (INVENTORY NUMBER 05341)

COURTESY JAN KRUGIER GALLERY, NEW YORK

23.8.50.

FIGURE 44

MATERNITÉ

1951, PENCIL ON PAPER, 10 5/8 X 8 1/4 INCHES (27 X 21 CM)

MARINA PICASSO COLLECTION (INVENTORY NUMBER 05324)

COURTESY JAN KRUGIER GALLERY, NEW YORK

28.2.54.
III261

FIGURE 48

VISAGE À DEUX PROFILS

1959, INDIA INK ON PAPER, 8 1/4 X 10 5/8 INCHES (21 X 27 CM)

MARINA PICASSO COLLECTION (INVENTORY NUMBER 06373)

COURTESY JAN KRUGIER GALLERY, NEW YORK

IV

FIGURE 51

HOMME À LA SAUTERELLE ET NU COUCHE

1969, CRAYON ON PAPER, 21 3/8 X 27 5/8 INCHES (54.3 X 70.2 CM)

PRIVATE COLLECTION

FIGURE 53

FEMMES

1971, PENCIL ON PAPER, 14 5/8 X 12 5/8 INCHES (37 X 32 CM)

COURTESY JAN KRUGIER GALLERY, NEW YORK

12.5.72.II

LIST OF WORKS

FIGURE 1
CHANTEUSE (RECTO)
TÊTE D'ESPAGNOLE (VERSO)
1899-1900, PASTEL ON PAPER, 6 1/4 X 3 1/2 INCHES (16.5 X 9.5 CM)
SIGNED LOWER LEFT VERSO: *P.R. Picasso*
NUMBERED AND DATED LOWER RIGHT VERSO: *1121 PP 1900/1121/30*
MARINA PICASSO COLLECTION (INVENTORY NUMBER 00245)
COURTESY JAN KRUGIER GALLERY, NEW YORK

FIGURE 2
ETUDE DE PERSONNAGES (ETUDE POUR "COMPOSITION: LES PAYSANS")
1906, WATERCOLOR AND SANGUINE ON PAPER, 11 3/4 X 9 1/4 INCHES
(30 X 23.5 CM)
ZERVOS VOL. XXII, NO. 349
MARINA PICASSO COLLECTION (INVENTORY NUMBER 00728)
COURTESY JAN KRUGIER GALLERY, NEW YORK

FIGURE 3
FEMME AU CHAPEAU À PLUME
1919, GOUACHE ON PAPER, 6 1/2 X 4 1/4 INCHES (16.5 X 11 CM)
MARINA PICASSO COLLECTION (INVENTORY NUMBER 02556)
COURTESY JAN KRUGIER GALLERY, NEW YORK

FIGURE 4
GUÉRIDON ET GUITARE
1920, GOUACHE ON PAPER, 10 7/8 X 8 1/4 INCHES (27.5 X 21 CM)
DATED VERSO: *25.8.20*
MARINA PICASSO COLLECTION (INVENTORY NUMBER 02787)
COURTESY JAN KRUGIER GALLERY, NEW YORK

FIGURE 5
NATURE MORTE AU GUÉRIDON
1920, JUAN-LES-PINS, OIL ON CANVAS, 45 3/4 X 28 1/2 INCHES
(119 X 76 CM)
MARINA PICASSO COLLECTION (INVENTORY NUMBER 12249)
COURTESY JAN KRUGIER GALLERY, NEW YORK

FIGURE 6
FEMME ASSISE
1920, JUAN-LES-PINS, GOUACHE, 10 3/4 X 8 3/8 INCHES (27.3 X 21.3 CM)
SIGNED LOWER RIGHT: *Picasso*
PRIVATE COLLECTION

FIGURE 7
COUPLE (CLASSICAL)
1924-25, INK AND WHITE GOUACHE ON PAPER, 22 X 28 1/4 INCHES
(55.9 X 71.8 CM)
INSCRIBED LOWER LEFT: *Pour Mon Ami Zervos*
SIGNED LOWER LEFT: *Picasso*
PRIVATE COLLECTION

FIGURE 8
ETUDE POUR LYSISTRATA
1933, PENCIL ON PAPER, 10 5/8 X 7 1/8 INCHES (27 X 18 CM)
MARINA PICASSO COLLECTION (INVENTORY NUMBER 03517)
COURTESY JAN KRUGIER GALLERY, NEW YORK

FIGURE 9
VASE DE FLEURS
1936, WATERCOLOR AND COLORED PENCILS ON PAPER, 10 X 6 3/4 INCHES
(25.5 X 17 CM)
DATED LOWER RIGHT: *21 Fevrier XXXVI*
MARINA PICASSO COLLECTION (INVENTORY NUMBER 03742)
COURTESY JAN KRUGIER GALLERY, NEW YORK

FIGURE 10
HOMME AU BERET (LE MARIN)
1946, WATERCOLOR, 19 3/4 X 13 INCHES (50.5 X 33 CM)
PRIVATE COLLECTION

FIGURE 11
ETUDE POUR "LE CHANT DES FLEURS"
1955, COLORED PENCILS ON PAPER, 10 5/8 X 8 1/4 INCHES (27 X 21 CM)
NUMBERED AND DATED UPPER RIGHT: *XV 19.28.9.55.*
ZERVOS VOL. XVI, NO. 43
MARINA PICASSO COLLECTION (INVENTORY NUMBER 05680)
COURTESY JAN KRUGIER GALLERY, NEW YORK

FIGURE 12
ETUDE POR "LE CHANT DES FLEURS"
1955, COLORED PENCILS ON PAPER, 9 1/2 X 8 1/4 INCHES (27 X 21 CM)
NUMBERED AND DATED UPPER RIGHT: *XVI 19.26.9.55.*
ZERVOS VOL. XVI, NO. 444
MARINA PICASSO COLLECTION (INVENTORY NUMBER 05681)
COURTESY JAN KRUGIER GALLERY, NEW YORK

FIGURE 13
TÊTES D'HOMME ET DE FEMME
1970, FELT PEN ON PAPER, 11 X 3 1/2 INCHES (27.5 X 21 CM)
SIGNED LOWER LEFT: *Picasso*
ZERVOS VOL. XXXII, NO. 315
PRIVATE COLLECTION

FIGURE 14
DEUX FEMMES NUES DEBOUT
1971, PENCIL AND RED CRAYON ON PAPER, 12 1/4 X 9 5/8 INCHES
(31 X 24.5 CM)
DATED AND NUMBERED UPPER LEFT: *Samedi 11.12.71.II*
DATED LOWER RIGHT: *Samedi 11.12.71.*
SIGNED LOWER RIGHT: *Picasso*
STAMPED AND NUMBERED LOWER RIGHT: *Collection Nounours - M&J Bresnau
No. 38*
COURTESY JAN KRUGIER GALLERY, NEW YORK

FIGURE 15
FEMME ET FLEURS
1971, PENCIL AND RED CRAYON ON PAPER, 14 5/8 X 12 5/8 INCHES
(37 X 32 CM)
DATED AND NUMBERED UPPER RIGHT: *12.12.71.V*
STAMPED AND NUMBERED LOWER RIGHT: *Collection Nounours - M&J Bresnau
No. 55*
COURTESY JAN KRUGIER GALLERY, NEW YORK

FIGURE 16
FEMME ET FLEURS
1971, PENCIL AND RED CRAYON ON PAPER, 14 5/8 X 12 5/8 INCHES
(37 X 32 CM)
DATED AND NUMBERED UPPER LEFT: *12.12.71.III*
STAMPED AND NUMBERED LOWER RIGHT: *Collection Nounours - M&J Bresnau
No. 53*
COURTESY JAN KRUGIER GALLERY, NEW YORK.

FIGURE 17
DEUX FEMMES EN CHAPEAU
1901, BLACK INK ON PAPER, 12 /4 X 7 7/8 INCHES (31 X 20 CM)
MARINA PICASSO COLLECTION (INVENTORY NUMBER 00300)
COURTESY JAN KRUGIER GALLERY, NEW YORK

FIGURE 18
PORTRAIT DE PACO SANCHA (RECTO)
FEMME NUE (VERSO)
1901, 14 3/8 X 9 7/8 INCHES (36.5 X 25.5 CM)
INK WASH ON PAPER (RECTO)
CHARCOAL ON PAPER (VERSO)
DATED AND INSCRIBED UPPER LEFT RECTO: *1079PP/Portrait de Mon Ami Paco
Sancha Dessinateur espagnol*
DATED AND NUMBERED LOWER RIGHT VERSO: *221/298 et 300 1121/95
1901*
ZERVOS VOL. XXI, NO. 300 (RECTO)
ZERVOS VOL. XXI, NO. 298 (VERSO)
MARINA PICASSO COLLECTION (INVENTORY NUMBER 00475)
COURTESY JAN KRUGIER GALLERY, NEW YORK.

FIGURE 19
NU COUCHÉ (RECTO)
DEUX ÉTUDES DE DANSEUSES (VERSO)
1901, 12 5/8 X 10 5/8 INCHES (32.5 X 27 CM)
CONTÉ CRAYON ON PAPER (RECTO)
INDIA INK ON PAPER (VERSO)
DATED AND NUMBERED LOWER LEFT VERSO: *1901 221/272 et 271 1121*
NUMBERED CENTER VERSO: *1073PP*
ZERVOS VOL. XXI, NO. 273 (RECTO)
ZERVOS VOL. XXI, NO. 272 (VERSO)
MARINA PICASSO COLLECTION (INVENTORY NUMBER 00476)
COURTESY JAN KRUGIER GALLERY, NEW YORK

FIGURE 20
PORTRAIT DE JEUNE FILLE
1903, PENCIL ON PAPER, 12 5/8 X 8 5/8 INCHES (32 X 22 CM)
SIGNED LOWER LEFT: *PICASSO*
ZERVOS VOL. XXII, NO. 35
PRIVATE COLLECTION

FIGURE 21
COLOMBINE (ETUDE POUR "LES NOCES DE PIERRETTE")
1905, PENCIL ON PAPER, 12 1/4 X 7 7/8 INCHES (31 X 20 CM)
ACCOMPANIED BY A CERTIFICATE OF AUTHENTICITY FROM MONSIEUR PIERRE
DAIX, SIGNED OCTOBER 11, 1989, PARIS
ZERVOS VOL. XXII, NO. 147
MARINA PICASSO COLLECTION (INVENTORY NUMBER 00656)
COURTESY JAN KRUGIER GALLERY, NEW YORK

FIGURE 22
NU
1908-1909, INDIA INK ON PAPER, 12 5/8 X 9 1/2 INCHES (32 X 24 CM)
ZERVOS VOL. XXVI, NO. 382
MARINA PICASSO COLLECTION (INVENTORY NUMBER 01095)
COURTESY JAN KRUGIER GALLERY, NEW YORK

FIGURE 23
NATURE MORTE À LA TASSE
1909-1910, GRAPHITE ON PAPER, 10 5/8 X 8 1/4 INCHES (27 X 21 CM)
MARINA PICASSO COLLECTION (INVENTORY NUMBER 01134)
COURTESY JAN KRUGIER GALLERY, NEW YORK

FIGURE 24
VIOLIN SUR UNE TABLE RONDE
1913, GRAPHITE ON PAPER, 4 3/8 X 6 3/4 INCHES (21 X 27.5 CM)
NUMBERED LOWER LEFT: *1065 PP*
ZERVOS VOL. XXVIII, NO. 334
MARINA PICASSO COLLECTION (INVENTORY NUMBER 01524)
COURTESY JAN KRUGIER GALLERY, NEW YORK

FIGURE 25
STILL LIFE WITH BOTTLE
1913-14, PENCIL ON CREAM PAPER, 19 1/2 X 14 7/8 INCHES
(49.5 X 37.7 CM)
SIGNED UPPER LEFT VERSO: *PICASSO*
PRIVATE COLLECTION

FIGURE 26
HOMME DANS UN FAUTEUIL
1914, PENCIL ON PAPER, 11 3/4 X 7 7/8 INCHES (30 X 20 CM)
MARINA PICASSO COLLECTION (INVENTORY NUMBER 01816)
COURTESY JAN KRUGIER GALLERY, NEW YORK

FIGURE 27
HOMME AU CHAPEAU
1915, PENCIL ON PAPER, 12 X 8 INCHES (30 X 20 CM)
ZERVOS VOL. XXIX, NO. 126
MARINA PICASSO COLLECTION (INVENTORY NUMBER 01708)
COURTESY JAN KRUGIER GALLERY, NEW YORK

FIGURE 28
TÊTE DE FEMME COUCHÉE (ELVIRA PALADINI)
1915-1916, PENCIL ON PAPER, 12 1/4 X 8 1/2 INCHES (31 X 21.5 CM)
NUMBERED LOWER LEFT: *1116/10*
ZERVOS VOL. XXIX, NO. 196 (DIMENSIONS REVERSED)
MARINA PICASSO COLLECTION (INVENTORY NUMBER 02081)
COURTESY JAN KRUGIER GALLERY, NEW YORK

FIGURE 29
ETUDE POUR UN PORTRAIT DE FEMME ASSISE (RECTO)
NU DEBOUT (VERSO)
1915-1916, PARIS, PENCIL ON PAPER, 12 1/4 X 7 1/2 INCHES (31 X 19 CM)
NUMBERED UPPER LEFT RECTO: *2552*
NUMBERED LOWER LEFT VERSO: *443P*
DATED AND NUMBERED UPPER LEFT VERSO: *26.1283.1915 1148/13D*
ZERVOS VOL. VI, NO. 1283 (RECTO)
MARINA PICASSO COLLECTION (INVENTORY NUMBER 02426)
COURTESY JAN KRUGIER GALLERY, NEW YORK

FIGURE 30
NU DEBOUT, LES PIEDS DANS L'EAU
1920, PENCIL ON PAPER, 9 1/4 X 4 1/2 INCHES (23 X 11.5 CM)
MARINA PICASSO COLLECTION (INVENTORY NUMBER 02935)
COURTESY JAN KRUGIER GALLERY, NEW YORK

FIGURE 31
LES TROIS GRÂCES
1923, INDIA INK ON LETTERHEAD FROM THE "CAP D'ANTIBES" HOTEL,
10 5/8 X 8 5/8 INCHES (27 X 22 CM)
MARINA PICASSO COLLECTION (INVENTORY NUMBER 03171)
COURTESY JAN KRUGIER GALLERY, NEW YORK

FIGURE 32
BAIGNEUSE (CARNET 67, P. 2)
1923, INDIA INK ON PAPER, 10 3/8 X 14 3/8 INCHES (26.5 X 36.5 CM)
MARINA PICASSO COLLECTION (INVENTORY NUMBER 08726)
COURTESY JAN KRUGIER GALLERY, NEW YORK

FIGURE 33
BAIGNEUSES (CARNET 67, P. 7)
1923, INDIA INK ON PAPER, 10 3/8 X 14 3/8 INCHES (26.5 X 36.5 CM)
MARINA PICASSO COLLECTION (INVENTORY NUMBER 08731)
COURTESY JAN KRUGIER GALLERY, NEW YORK

FIGURE 34
BAIGNEUSES (CARNET 67, P. 8)
1923, INDIA INK ON PAPER, 10 3/8 X 14 3/8 INCHES (26.5 X 36.5 CM)
MARINA PICASSO COLLECTION (INVENTORY NUMBER 08732)
COURTESY JAN KRUGIER GALLERY, NEW YORK

FIGURE 35
TÊTE DE FEMME (CARNET 67, P. 15)
1923, INDIA INK ON PAPER, 10 3/8 X 14 3/8 INCHES (36.5 X 26.5 CM)
MARINA PICASSO COLLECTION (INVENTORY NUMBER 08739)
COURTESY JAN KRUGIER GALLERY, NEW YORK

FIGURE 36
VISAGE DE FEMME
1924, PENCIL ON PAPER, 5 1/2 X 4 1/4 INCHES (14 X 10.5 CM)
CF. ZERVOS VOL. V, NO. 269-273
MARINA PICASSO COLLECTION (INVENTORY NUMBER 03219)
COURTESY JAN KRUGIER GALLERY, NEW YORK

FIGURE 37
ETUDE POUR LYSISTRATA–DIVERS PERSONNAGES
1933, PENCIL ON PAPER, 7 1/2 X 10 5/8 INCHES (19 X 27 CM)
MARINA PICASSO COLLECTION (INVENTORY NUMBER 03598)
COURTESY JAN KRUGIER GALLERY, NEW YORK

FIGURE 38
FLÛTISTE ASSISE ET DORMEUSE
1933, INDIA INK ON PAPER, 6 1/4 X 8 5/8 INCHES (16 X 22 CM)
MARINA PICASSO COLLECTION (INVENTORY NUMBER 03643)
COURTESY JAN KRUGIER GALLERY, NEW YORK

FIGURE 39
VISAGE
1941, PEN AND INDIA INK ON PAPER, 10 5/8 X 8 1/4 INCHES (27 X 21 CM)
DATED UPPER LEFT: 16 juillet 41
ZERVOS VOL. XI, NO. 286
MARINA PICASSO COLLECTION (INVENTORY NUMBER 04161)
COURTESY JAN KRUGIER GALLERY, NEW YORK

FIGURE 40
FEMME ALLONGÉE
1941, PENCIL ON PAPER, 8 1/4 X 10 5/8 INCHES (21 X 27 CM)
DATED UPPER RIGHT: 26 Août 41
ZERVOS, VOL. XI, NO. 260
MARINA PICASSO COLLECTION (INVENTORY NUMBER 04235)
COURTESY JAN KRUGIER GALLERY, NEW YORK

FIGURE 41
FEMME ALLONGÉE SUR UN LIT
1941, PENCIL ON PAPER, 8 1/4 X 10 5/8 INCHES (21 X 27 CM)
DATED UPPER RIGHT: 26 Août 41
MARINA PICASSO COLLECTION (INVENTORY NUMBER 04234)
COURTESY JAN KRUGIER GALLERY, NEW YORK

FIGURE 42
NU
1946, PENCIL ON PAPER, 26 1/8 X 19 7/8 INCHES (66.5 X 50.5 CM)
DATED UPPER RIGHT: 30.12.46.
ZERVOS, VOL. XIV, NO. 347
MARINA PICASSO COLLECTION (INVENTORY NUMBER 04942)
COURTESY JAN KRUGIER GALLERY, NEW YORK

FIGURE 43
PORTRAIT
1950, PENCIL ON PAPER, 25 3/4 X 19 7/8 INCHES (65.5 X 50.5 CM)
DATED UPPER LEFT: 23.8.50
MARINA PICASSO COLLECTION (INVENTORY NUMBER 05341)
COURTESY JAN KRUGIER GALLERY, NEW YORK

FIGURE 44
MATERNITÉ
1951, PENCIL ON PAPER, 10 5/8 X 8 1/4 INCHES (27 X 21 CM)
NUMBERED AND DATED UPPER RIGHT: 5.1.51.V
MARINA PICASSO COLLECTION (INVENTORY NUMBER 05324)
COURTESY JAN KRUGIER GALLERY, NEW YORK

FIGURE 45
MATERNITÉ
1954, PENCIL ON PAPER, 10 5/8 X 8 1/4 INCHES (27 X 21 CM)
NUMBERED AND DATED UPPER RIGHT: 5.1.51.VI
MARINA PICASSO COLLECTION (INVENTORY NUMBER 05325)
COURTESY JAN KRUGIER GALLERY, NEW YORK

FIGURE 46
NU COUCHÉ ENDORMI
1954, PENCIL ON PAPER, 9 1/2 X 12 5/8 INCHES (24 X 32 CM)
DATED AND NUMBERED UPPER LEFT: 28.2.54.VII
ZERVOS, VOL. XVI, NO. 244
MARINA PICASSO COLLECTION (INVENTORY NUMBER 05633)
COURTESY JAN KRUGIER GALLERY, NEW YORK

FIGURE 47
NU COUCHÉ ENDORMI
1954, PENCIL ON PAPER, 8 1/4 X 10 5/8 INCHES (21 X 27 CM)
DATED AND NUMBERED UPPER LEFT: 28.2.54.III
ZERVOS, VOL. XVI, NO. 249
MARINA PICASSO COLLECTION (INVENTORY NUMBER 05629)
COURTESY JAN KRUGIER GALLERY, NEW YORK

FIGURE 48
VISAGE À DEUX PROFILS
1959, INDIA INK ON PAPER, 8 1/4 X 10 5/8 INCHES (21 X 27 CM)
DATED VERSO: 11.7.59.VI
MARINA PICASSO COLLECTION (INVENTORY NUMBER 06373)
COURTESY JAN KRUGIER GALLERY, NEW YORK

FIGURE 49
POUR GAGARINE
1961, PENCIL ON PAPER, 13 X 16 1/2 INCHES (33 X 42 CM)
INSCRIBED LOWER CENTER: Youri Gagarine
NUMBERED LOWER LEFT: IV
ZERVOS, VOL. XIX, NO. 444
MARINA PICASSO COLLECTION (INVENTORY NUMBER 06134)
COURTESY JAN KRUGIER GALLERY, NEW YORK

FIGURE 50
ETUDE POUR (L'ENLÈVEMENT DES SABINES)
1963, PENCIL ON PAPER, 4 1/4 X 8 7/8 INCHES (10.5 X 22.5 CM)
DATED AND NUMBERED LOWER RIGHT: 11.3.63.IV
ZERVOS, VOL. XXIII, NO. 184
MARINA PICASSO COLLECTION (INVENTORY NUMBER 06208)
COURTESY JAN KRUGIER GALLERY, NEW YORK

FIGURE 51

HOMME À LA SAUTERELLE ET NU COUCHE

1969, CRAYON ON PAPER, 21 3/8 X 70 5/8 INCHES (54.3 X 70.2 CM)
SIGNED AND DATED LOWER RIGHT: *Picasso 17.11.69.III*
PRIVATE COLLECTION

FIGURE 52

DEUX FEMMES ASSISES

1971, INK ON PAPER, 9 3/8 X 12 5/8 INCHES (23.7 X 32 CM)
DATED AND NUMBERED UPPER LEFT: *25.X.26.4.71.I*
SIGNED UPPER LEFT: *Picasso*
STAMPED AND NUMBERED LOWER LEFT: *Collection Nounours - M&J Bresnau
No. 25*
COURTESY JAN KRUGIER GALLERY, NEW YORK

FIGURE 53

FEMMES

1971, PENCIL ON PAPER, 14 5/8 X 12 5/8 INCHES (37 X 32 CM)
DATED UPPER RIGHT: *25.12.71.*
STAMPED LOWER LEFT: *Collection Nounours - M&J Bresnau No. 38* AND NUM-
BERED: *45*
COURTESY JAN KRUGIER GALLERY, NEW YORK

FIGURE 54

LE GALANT MOUSQUETAIRE

1972, PENCIL, INDIA INK, AND INK WASH ON PAPER, 12 1/4 X 16 INCHES
(31.1 X 40.6 CM)
DATED AND NUMBERED LOWER RIGHT: *12.5.72.II*
ZERVOS, VOL. XXXIII, NO. 384
MARINA PICASSO COLLECTION (INVENTORY NUMBER 06303)
COURTESY JAN KRUGIER GALLERY, NEW YORK